ZIHUATANEJO,

MÉXICO

TRAVEL GUIDE

2023 - 2024

The Definitive Guide to one of Mexico's most intriguing places with gorgeous hidden beauty.

Kenneth Finley

D1522254

Copyright

Kenneth Finley © 2023. All rights reserved

Before this document is duplicated or reproduced in any manner, the publisher's consent must be gained.

Therefore, the contents within can neither be stored electronically, transferred, nor kept in a database. Neither in part nor in full can the document be copied, scanned, faxed, or retained without approval from the publisher or creator.

TABLE OF CONTENTS

About This Guide

Welcome to your necessary companion for visiting the gorgeous seaside beauty of Zihuatanejo, Mexico in 2023-2024. This expertly created travel book is meant to be your go-to resource for an outstanding time in one of Mexico's most intriguing places.

Why Choose This Guide?

In a sea of travel information, this book stands out for its up-to-date suggestions and deep observations. Here's what makes it apart:

- **Current Information**: We recognise that travel is dynamic, and what was true yesterday may not be the case today. This book is constantly updated to reflect the newest changes, ensuring you have the most current and relevant information at your fingertips.

- Local Expertise: Our team of travel specialists has researched Zihuatanejo to provide you with true, insider suggestions. We've visited the hidden beauties, eaten at the local hotspots, and unearthed the best-kept secrets to make your vacation unique.

- **Comprehensive Coverage:** Whether you're a beach lover, history buff, gourmet, or adventure seeker, this book caters to all sorts of tourists. From comprehensive itineraries to practical recommendations, we've got you covered.

What You'll Find Inside

Whether you have a week or longer to spend, we provide expertly tailored itineraries to help you make the most of your stay in Zihuatanejo.

- **Insider Tips:** Discover off-the-beaten-path sights, money-saving tricks, and sustainable travel habits to enrich your vacation.

- **Accommodation and Dining Recommendations**: From luxury resorts to budget-friendly alternatives, we share insights on where to stay and where to sample the finest local and international food.

- **Practical Information**: Find vital travel data, like visa needs, safety tips, and transit alternatives, to ensure a flawless journey.

- **Festival and Event Highlights:** Don't miss out on Zihuatanejo's lively culture. We highlight the yearly festivals and events that give a particular flavor to your stay.

Embark on your Zihuatanejo vacation equipped with this guide's skills. Whether you're a first-time visitor or returning to this tropical paradise, let our insights be your compass as you discover the sun-kissed beaches, rich history, and friendly hospitality that make Zihuatanejo a must-visit destination.

Prepare to immerse yourself in the beauty and culture of Zihuatanejo, and let this guide be your loyal friend during your vacation. Your Mexican journey begins here!

Chapter 1: INTRODUCTION

1.1. Welcome to Zihuatanejo

Nestled on the Pacific Coast of Mexico, Zihuatanejo provides a stunning combination of natural beauty, rich culture, and friendly hospitality that lures people from across the globe. This introduction serves as your entryway to this lovely place, giving insights into why Zihuatanejo should be at the top of your trip list, key preparation recommendations, and a primer on getting about.

1.2. Why Visit Zihuatanejo?

Zihuatanejo, frequently referred to as "Zihua" by the locals, is a paradise for visitors seeking a genuine Mexican experience. Here are strong reasons to pick Zihuatanejo as your next holiday spot:

- **Idyllic Beaches**: Zihuatanejo is famed for its gorgeous beaches. Playa La Ropa, with its golden sands and crystal-clear seas, is a sunbather's dream. Playa Principal and Playa Madera provide a vibrant scene with lots of activities and seaside eating.

- **Charming Fishing community**: Unlike its glamorous neighbor, Ixtapa, Zihuatanejo preserves the beauty of a classic Mexican fishing community. The town's cobblestone walkways, colorful markets, and friendly residents create a genuine and laid-back vibe.

- **Cultural Richness**: Immerse yourself in the local culture by touring Zihuatanejo's art galleries, attending traditional festivals, and seeing the town's historic landmarks. Don't miss the opportunity to observe the brilliant colors and sounds of Mexican festivals.

- **Delectable Cuisine**: Zihuatanejo has a diversity of eating alternatives, from seaside seafood shacks to upmarket international eateries.Savour scrumptious delicacies like ceviche, grilled seafood, and tacos while enjoying breathtaking seaside views.

- **Water Adventures**: Whether you're into snorkeling, scuba diving, fishing, or sailing, Zihuatanejo provides a plethora of water-based activities. Explore the undersea world of the Pacific Ocean or set sail on a sunset cruise.

1.3. Travel Planning Tips

Before you begin on your Zihuatanejo tour, consider these useful planning tips:

Ideal Time to Visit: Zihuatanejo boasts a tropical environment, with November to April being the dry season and the ideal time to visit. May through October delivers intermittent rain showers, but the beautiful scenery is a trade-off for some afternoon rain.

- **Travel Documents**: Ensure you have a valid passport and verify the visa requirements for your country of residence Mexico may grant visa-free entrance or need a tourist visa depending on your nationality.

- **Currency and Language**: The Mexican Peso (MXN) is the native currency. While many stores take US dollars, it's recommended to carry some pesos for little transactions. Spanish is the official language, however, you'll find English spoken in tourist areas.

- **Health Precautions**: Consider travel insurance, and verify if any vaccines are advised for your trip. Zihuatanejo offers good medical services, however, it's vital to be prepared.

1.4. Getting Around

Navigating Zihuatanejo and its surrounds is pretty easy:

- **Walking**: The town of Zihuatanejo is pedestrian-friendly, letting you explore its picturesque streets, marketplaces, and beaches on foot. Comfortable walking shoes are advised.

- **Taxis:** Taxis are frequently accessible and are a handy method to move about town and to surrounding locations like Ixtapa. Be careful to agree on the fare with the driver before heading out.

- **Public Transportation:** Local buses, known as "combis," offer a cheap means to travel within Zihuatanejo and to surrounding cities. They are generally vibrant and simple to notice.

- **Automobile Rentals**: If you want to explore the area extensively, automobile rentals are available. Be prepared for

Mexican traffic regulations and road conditions.

As you prepare to begin your Zihuatanejo vacation, keep these introductory observations in mind. With its combination of natural beauty, cultural depth, and friendly friendliness, Zihuatanejo guarantees an outstanding vacation experience. This book will follow you on your trip, giving in-depth advice and insights to guarantee your visit to Zihuatanejo is nothing short of exceptional.

Chapter 2: ZIHUATANEJO AT A GLANCE

2.1. Geography and Climate

Zihuatanejo's landscape is nothing short of breathtaking. Situated along the Pacific Coast of Mexico, this coastal jewel features spectacular scenery that effortlessly merges the verdant Sierra Madre del Sur mountains with the turquoise seas of the Pacific Ocean. Its position inside the state of Guerrero placed it amid a zone of natural beauty that few locations can equal.

The climate in Zihuatanejo is tropical and lovely. The dry season, from November to April, delivers bright days and pleasant nights, making it the best period for vacationers. During these months, anticipate temperatures

17

in the mid-80s to low 90s Fahrenheit (about 29-35°C). The wet season, from May to October, sees intermittent rainfall, which feeds the rich vegetation and contributes to the town's lush beauty.

2.2. History and Culture

Zihuatanejo has a rich history that dates back to prehistoric times. The area was inhabited by indigenous peoples long before Spanish colonialism, and elements of their culture may still be observed in the region's art and rituals.

During colonial times, Zihuatanejo functioned as an important port for commerce between Mexico and the Philippines. Its name even stems from the Nahuatl term "Cihuatlan," which means "Place of Women" - a reference to the female goddesses adored by the original people.

Today, Zihuatanejo is a dynamic combination of indigenous, Spanish, and contemporary Mexican culture. Its streets are adorned with , and its plazas host traditional festivals and marketplaces. The inhabitants of Zihuatanejo are friendly and inviting, making it simple for tourists to immerse themselves in the native way of life.

2.3. Local Cuisine and Drinks

Zihuatanejo's culinary scene is a delicious combination of Mexican tastes, fresh seafood, and cosmopolitan influences. When eating in Zihuatanejo, you'll discover an assortment of scrumptious options:

- **Seafood Delights**: With its beachfront position, Zihuatanejo is a seafood lover's heaven. Try the catch of the day, whether it's snapper, dorado, or lobster, cooked with native seasonings and served at coastal palapas or upmarket restaurants.

- **Tacos and Tamales**: Savor traditional Mexican street cuisine with tacos packed with marinated meats, fresh salsa, and homemade tamales. Be sure to taste the local favorite, "Tacos de Pescado" (fish tacos).

- **Traditional Dishes**: Sample regional favorites like "Pozole," a substantial soup, or "Mole," a thick and savory sauce. These recipes provide a flavor of Mexican culture.

- **Refreshing Beverages:** Cool off with "Agua Frescas," which are fruity, non-alcoholic beverages, or enjoy a cool Mexican beer like Pacifico or Modelo. Don't forget to sip on a "Margarita" prepared with local tequila.

Zihuatanejo's culinary scene represents the town's rich cultural legacy, where old traditions meet contemporary influences. Whether you're eating the finest seafood on the beach or relishing traditional Mexican meals, Zihuatanejo provides a wonderful gastronomic excursion.

In this chapter, you've received a peek at Zihuatanejo's stunning terrain, climate, and cultural legacy, as well as a taste of its variety and wonderful food. As you explore further into your Zihuatanejo tour, these insights will deepen your enjoyment of this unique place.

Chapter 3: PRACTICAL INFORMATION

3.1 Travel Essentials (Visas, Currency, Language)

Before going on your trip to Zihuatanejo, it's vital to have your travel needs in order:

- **Visas:** Most travelers to Mexico, including residents from the United States, Canada, the European Union, and many other countries, do not require a visa for stays of up to 180 days for tourist reasons. However, it's vital to examine Mexico's visa requirements depending on your country and travel purpose before your trip.

- **Currency**: The official currency of Zihuatanejo is the Mexican Peso (MXN). While some shops take US dollars, it's good to carry some pesos for little purchases, local markets, and tipping. Currency exchange services are offered at airports and banks.

- **Language**: Spanish is the official language of Mexico, including Zihuatanejo. While many individuals in the tourist business understand English, it's essential to know some basic Spanish phrases to improve your experience and engage with locals.

3.2. Safety Tips

Zihuatanejo is considered a safe place for vacationers. However, like any other area in the globe, it's vital to adopt common-sense safety precautions:

- **Personal possessions:** Keep a watch on your possessions, particularly in busy settings or on public transit. Use hotel safes for passports, valuables, and extra cash.

- **Beach Safety**: While Zihuatanejo's beaches are magnificent, it's essential to observe caution signs. Strong currents may make swimming risky, so always heed lifeguards' directions and swim in specified locations.

- **Health and cleanliness**: Ensure you keep hydrated, apply sunscreen, and practice basic cleanliness. Carry a tiny first-aid kit for minor cuts or scratches.

- **Local Laws and Customs**: Respect local laws and customs, especially those relating to drug use, and be aware of local rules while taking part in water sports.

- **Emergency Services**: Familiarize yourself with emergency contact numbers, including the tourist police, local hospitals, and the closest embassy or consulate of your country.

3.3. Health and Medical Services

Zihuatanejo has reputable medical services, however, it's necessary to keep aware and prepared for any health-related situations:

- **Travel Insurance**: Consider obtaining travel insurance that covers medical emergencies and evacuation. Check whether your current insurance covers international coverage.

- **Immunisations**: Consult your healthcare physician or a travel clinic for recommended immunisations before flying to Mexico. Common immunisations include Hepatitis A and B, typhoid, and tetanus.

- **Pharmacies**: Zihuatanejo offers well-stocked pharmacies where you may get over-the-counter and prescription drugs. Pharmacists are typically informed and may give help.

- **Medical Facilities**: In case of a medical emergency, Zihuatanejo contains medical clinics and hospitals. The Red Cross is also ready for emergency aid.

3.4. Communication and Internet

Staying connected while in Zihuatanejo is straightforward:

- **Mobile Network:** Mexico offers a solid mobile network, and you can acquire local SIM cards or international roaming plans from your own country.

- **Wi-Fi:** Many hotels, restaurants, and cafés in Zihuatanejo provide free Wi-Fi connectivity. It's a good idea to check with your hotel about Wi-Fi availability and passwords.

- **Internet Cafes**: While becoming less prevalent, you may still locate internet cafes in Zihuatanejo if you require a computer and internet connection.

- **Postal Services**: Zihuatanejo offers post offices where you may send postcards or letters, but remember that international postage might be pricey.

By being aware of these practical factors, you'll ensure a smoother and more pleasurable experience throughout your vacation to Zihuatanejo. Whether you're addressing travel needs, prioritizing safety, or keeping connected, this chapter gives you the information required to negotiate the practical parts of your trip.

Chapter 4: ACCOMMODATION

One of the crucial components of organizing your vacation to Zihuatanejo is picking the proper lodging. This chapter digs into the vast variety of solutions available, catering to varying tastes and budgets.

4.1. Top Hotels and Resorts

Zihuatanejo features an excellent range of top-notch hotels and resorts that provide elegance, comfort, and exquisite service. Here are a few prominent options:

- **Viceroy Zihuatanejo**: A five-star beachside resort that emanates luxury and calm. With beautiful gardens, private plunge pools, and breathtaking views of the bay, it's a favorite among honeymooners and couples seeking a romantic escape.

- **Thompson Zihuatanejo**: This boutique hotel mixes contemporary style with Mexican characteristics. Enjoy beachfront apartments, infinity pools, and a rooftop bar with magnificent views of Zihuatanejo Bay.

- **La Casa Que Canta**: Perched on a cliff overlooking the beach, this tiny, adults-only hotel is a jewel. Its Moroccan-inspired architecture, infinity pools, and outstanding restaurants make it a unique vacation.

- **Azul Ixtapa Grand Spa & Convention Center:** Located in adjacent Ixtapa, this all-inclusive resort provides an assortment of facilities, including a spa, various restaurants, and access to a private beach.

4.2. Budget-Friendly Options

For guests wishing to make the most of their money without compromising comfort, Zihuatanejo offers a selection of wallet-friendly accommodations:

- **Hostels**: Zihuatanejo offers various hostels with dormitory-style and private rooms, making it a good alternative for backpackers and lone travelers. They typically create a social environment and are a wonderful opportunity to meet other travelers.

- **Guesthouses and Bed & Breakfasts:** Quaint guesthouses and B&Bs are sprinkled around Zihuatanejo, providing quaint, locally managed lodgings with individualized service.

- **Small Hotels**: Look for smaller, family-run hotels and inns, particularly in the downtown area. These may give comfortable and economical choices within walking distance of the town's attractions.

- **Vacation Rentals**: Consider renting a private apartment or villa for extra room and amenities. Websites like Airbnb and VRBO provide several alternatives to pick from.

4.3. Vacation Rentals

Vacation rentals in Zihuatanejo are an increasingly popular alternative, particularly for those wanting more room, solitude, and a home-away-from-home experience. Here's what you may expect:

- **Variety of Options**: Vacation rentals come in numerous shapes, from modest apartments and seaside condominiums to huge villas with private pools. They cater to couples, families, and bigger groups.

- **Amenities**: Many vacation homes have fully furnished kitchens, living rooms, and outside spaces. This enables you to make your food, rest comfortably, and enjoy al fresco eating.

- **Local Experience**: Staying in a vacation rental typically gives a more genuine experience, enabling you to immerse yourself in the local culture and live like a Zihuatanejo native.

- **Flexibility**: You may select the location that fits you best, whether it's in the middle of the town, near the beach, or in a calmer residential neighborhood.

When selecting vacation rentals, be careful to check reviews, connect with hosts, and clarify any concerns you may have regarding the property to ensure a seamless booking experience.

In conclusion, Zihuatanejo provides a broad selection of hotel alternatives to suit all budgets and interests. Whether you're dreaming of a magnificent beachside resort, a modest guesthouse, or a private holiday rental,

Zihuatanejo's housing options are as varied as its natural beauty and cultural depth.

Chapter 5: THINGS TO DO IN ZIHUATANEJO

Zihuatanejo provides a diversity of activities and experiences to satisfy all travelers' preferences. From quiet beach days to vibrant evenings on the town, here's a complete guide to the finest things to do in this quaint seaside location.

5.1. Beaches and Water Activities

Zihuatanejo's major lure is its magnificent beaches and plentiful water sports. Here are some highlights:

- **Playa La Ropa**: This popular beach is perfect for swimming and sunbathing. The clean seas and calm waves make it great for families. You may also attempt paragliding, paddleboarding, or just chill in a seaside palapa café.

- **Playa Principal**: This bustling beach in the center of Zihuatanejo is home to various eateries providing fresh seafood. It's a center for boat cruises, including fishing expeditions and visits to adjacent islands.

- **Scuba Diving and Snorkeling:** Explore the underwater treasures of Zihuatanejo by diving or snorkeling. The warm Pacific seas are rich with colorful marine life, making it a delight for underwater aficionados.

- **Sailing & Sunset Cruises**: Enjoy a romantic sail into the sunset or go on a day cruise. Many companies offer these tours, replete with possibilities for snorkeling and tasty aboard meals.

5.2. Exploring the Town

Zihuatanejo's lovely town is a great spot to explore on foot. Highlights include:

- **Paseo del Pescador:** This lovely waterfront boulevard is dotted with restaurants, shops, and breathtaking views of Zihuatanejo Bay. It's the ideal area for a leisurely walk.

- **Mercado de Artesanías:** Visit the local craft market to find handcrafted textiles, ceramics, jew jewelry and other Mexican handicrafts. It's a fantastic area to pick from.

- **Iglesia de Nuestra Señora de Guadalupe:** Explore this gorgeous church in the center of Zihuatanejo, showcasing breathtaking architecture and a tranquil environment.

5.3. Shopping for Souvenirs

Zihuatanejo provides a broad choice of souvenirs, enabling you to carry a bit of Mexico home with you:

- **Artisan marketplaces**: Beyond the craft market, you'll discover numerous artisan marketplaces where you may buy traditional Mexican artifacts like Talavera pottery, embroidered linens, and handwoven baskets.

- **Local Art Galleries**: Zihuatanejo is home to various art galleries showing the work of brilliant local artists. You may discover paintings, sculptures, and other unique objects.

- **Jewellery Shops**: Mexico is known for its silver jewelry. Explore the town's jewelry stores to uncover lovely items created by local artists.

5.4. Nightlife and Entertainment

When the sun sets, Zihuatanejo comes alive with a dynamic nightlife scene:

- **Live Music**: Many restaurants and pubs provide live music, from traditional Mexican mariachi bands to modern performances. Enjoy a drink and dance the night away.

- **Cafes & Bars**: Zihuatanejo boasts a variety of bars and cafes where you may sip on drinks, sample local beers, and chat with other tourists.

- **Dance Clubs**: If you're in the mood for dancing, various clubs and discos keep the music flowing into the early hours.

Zihuatanejo's combination of natural beauty, cultural activities, and dynamic nightlife means there's something for everyone. Whether you're seeking leisure on the beach, cultural discovery, or exciting entertainment, Zihuatanejo guarantees an amazing trip.

Chapter 6: EXCURSIONS AND DAY TRIPS

Zihuatanejo provides an ideal location for thrilling excursions and day trips that enable you to discover the surrounding natural beauty, wildlife, and historical monuments. Here's a deeper look at some of the top options:

6.1. Ixtapa: Zihuatanejo's Neighbor

Ixtapa y Zihuatanejo's adjacent resort town, situated only a short drive away. While Zihuatanejo offers a delightful and genuine Mexican experience, Ixtapa delivers a more sophisticated and elegant setting. Here are some activities to consider:

- **Ixtapa Beaches**: Ixtapa features lovely beaches including Playa El Palmar, suitable for swimming and sunbathing. Many seaside resorts provide attractions including water sports, parasailing, and beachside bars.

- **Golf**: Golf lovers may tee off at the several golf courses in Ixtapa, which are recognised for their magnificent ocean vistas and tough fairways.

- **Marina Ixtapa:** Explore the marina, where you may hire boats for fishing expeditions, sunset cruises, or snorkeling experiences and Nature Tours

Zihuatanejo's natural surroundings are a paradise for animals and environment aficionados. Consider these ways to get closer to the local flora and fauna:

- **Ixtapa Island (Isla Ixtapa)**: Take a boat journey to Ixtapa Island, a natural park that's home to coral reefs, marine life, and a refuge for several bird species. Snorkeling and bird-watching are popular hobbies here.

- **Whale Watching**: From December to April, you may go on whale-watching cruises to observe the spectacular humpback whales during their migratory season.

- **El Refugio de Potosí:** Visit this ecological reserve and lagoon, which offers a refuge for crocodiles, birds, and other species. Guided excursions give informative insights into the local ecology.

6.2. Historical Sites Nearby

Explore the rich history of the area by visiting historical places within a short drive from Zihuatanejo:

- **Petatlán**: Located approximately 30 minutes from Zihuatanejo, Petatlán is home to the spectacular Iglesia de San Pedro Apostol, a church famed for its gold-plated altar. It's a fantastic site to learn about the local culture and history.

- **La Chole Archaeological Site:** Just over an hour's drive from Zihuatanejo, you may visit the ancient remains of La Chole, which date back to the pre-Hispanic era. This archaeological site looks into the area's indigenous past.

- **Troncones**: A short drive north of Zihuatanejo, Troncones is a quiet beach town famed for its surfing and calm ambience. It's a fantastic area to take a quiet day vacation and escape the hustle and bustle.

These excursions and day trips from Zihuatanejo offer different experiences, from experiencing the busy resort town of Ixtapa to immersing yourself in the region's natural beauty and rich history. Whether you're seeking adventure, leisure, or cultural discovery, the surroundings of Zihuatanejo have something to offer every sort of tourist.

Chapter 7: DINING AND CUISINE

Zihuatanejo's eating scene is a gourmet feast, presenting a fascinating blend of traditional Mexican tastes, exquisite seafood, and world cuisines. In this chapter, we'll examine the numerous gastronomic pleasures you may relish in Zihuatanejo.

7.1. Local Restaurants and Street Food

The essence of Zihuatanejo's gastronomic attraction rests in its local restaurants and street food sellers. These small eateries provide traditional Mexican meals that reflect the flavor of the area. Here's what to indulge in:

- **Tacos**: Street-side taco stalls are common in Zihuatanejo. Try "Tacos al Pastor," loaded with marinated pork, pineapple, and a choice of fresh salsas. Don't forget the lime!

- **Tamales**: These savory or sweet masa-based delicacies are commonly boiled in banana leaves and may be obtained at street sellers or local markets.

- **Ceviche**: Zihuatanejo's ceviche is noted for its freshness. Made from marinated seafood (typically fish or shrimp) with lime, cilantro, and chiles, it's a must-try seaside dish.

- **Enchiladas**: Savor these wrapped tortillas loaded with chicken, cheese, or other contents, covered with rich sauces and garnished with onions and crema.

- **Elotes and Esquites:** These street treats consist of corn on the cob () or kernels () coated with mayonnaise, cheese, lime, and chili powder—a delightful mix of tastes.

7.2. Seafood Specialties

Given its seaside setting, Zihuatanejo specializes in delivering seafood delicacies that will tickle your taste buds. Here are some seafood specialities to relish:

- **Pescado a la Talla**: Grilled fish, generally red snapper or sea bass, is coated in a delicious chili and garlic sauce. It's a spicy and flavorful pleasure.

- **Tostadas de Ceviche:** These crispy tortillas are topped with a large portion of ceviche, producing a pleasant and tangy snack or appetizer.

- **A la Plancha**: Grilled octopus is a delicacy in Zihuatanejo. Served tender and seasoned to perfection, it's a must-try for seafood fans.

- **Langosta (Lobster):** Zihuatanejo is famed for its lobster, which is commonly grilled, served with garlic butter, or integrated into numerous meals.

Sopa de Mariscos: Seafood soup packed with shrimp, fish, crab, and other treasures from the sea is a soothing and substantial meal.

7.3. International Dining Options

While Zihuatanejo specializes in traditional Mexican cuisine, it also provides foreign dining alternatives to appeal to varied preferences. Here are some foreign tastes to explore:

- **Italian**: You'll discover Italian trattorias providing pasta, pizza, and creamy risotto, complimented by exquisite wines.

- **French**: Experience French cuisine in beautiful bistros, where you can savor classics like coq au vin and escargot.

- **Asian Fusion**: Satisfy your appetites for Asian tastes with eateries serving sushi, Thai curries, and fusion meals.

- **International Fusion:** Many restaurants in Zihuatanejo fuse global influences, producing meals that seamlessly merge tastes from throughout the globe.

- **Vegetarian & Vegan**: Zihuatanejo is increasingly accepting dietary needs, with eateries providing plant-based alternatives and inventive vegetarian cuisine.

Zihuatanejo's eating scene provides a pleasant voyage through the vast world of Mexican and foreign food. Whether you're relishing the bright tastes of street cuisine, indulging in seafood delights, or exploring foreign dining alternatives, the town's culinary offerings are guaranteed to make a lasting impact on your taste buds.

Chapter 8: ZIHUATANEJO'S FESTIVALS AND EVENTS

Zihuatanejo's rich cultural legacy is honored throughout the year with a variety of exciting festivals and events. These events give a unique chance for guests to immerse themselves in local customs, music, dancing, and food. Here's a look into some of the yearly events and celebrations that make Zihuatanejo come alive:

- **Dia de la Candelaria (Candlemas Day):** This festive event takes place on February 2nd and symbolizes the conclusion of the Christmas season. It's a day when villagers dress up images of the baby Jesus from their nativity scenes and bring them to the church to be blessed. The streets are packed with processions, traditional dances, and tasty tamales.

- **Event of the Patron Saint of Zihuatanejo (Fiesta de San José):** Celebrated from March 15th to 19th, this event commemorates the patron saint of Zihuatanejo, Saint Joseph. The town comes alive with religious events, processions, fireworks, music, and dancing. It's a lively showcase of local religion and culture.

- **Semana Santa (Holy Week):** Holy Week, which happens in March or April, is one of the most prominent religious celebrations in Zihuatanejo. It involves processions, reenactments of the Passion of Christ, and special church services. It's a time for thought and devotion, with a celebratory atmosphere.

- **Independence Day (Dia de la Independencia):** September 16th is Mexico's Independence Day, and Zihuatanejo joins the country in celebrating with parades, music, dancing, and fireworks. The main plaza, or zócalo, is a focal point for the celebrations, with the customary "Grito de Dolores" (Cry of Dolores) at midnight.

- **Zihuatanejo International Guitar event:** Held yearly in March, this event brings together outstanding guitarists from throughout the globe. It's a week-long festival of music with concerts at different venues across Zihuatanejo, including the seashore.

- **Zihua SailFest**: An event that blends charity with pleasure, the Zihua SailFest takes place in early February. It involves sailboat races, live music, and many events to generate revenue for education and community initiatives.

- **Zihuatanejo Foreign Film Festival:** Typically held in January, this film festival features a mix of foreign and Mexican films. It's a chance for cinema aficionados to enjoy screenings, conversations, and contact with filmmakers.

- **Zihuatanejo Blues & Jazz event:** This yearly event takes place in March and boasts a roster of great performers playing blues and jazz music. It's a laid-back gathering with an intimate environment, frequently hosted on the beach.

These festivals and events give a unique glimpse into the heart and soul of Zihuatanejo. Whether you're a cultural enthusiast, music lover, or just want to experience the local customs, attending these events enables you to connect with the dynamic atmosphere of this picturesque seaside town.

Chapter 9: INSIDER TIPS

Traveling to Zihuatanejo is a chance to unearth hidden jewels, optimize your money, and adopt sustainable practices. In this chapter, we reveal exclusive recommendations that will improve your Zihuatanejo trip.

9.1. Hidden Gems & Off-the-Beaten-Path Attractions

While Zihuatanejo has its famed beaches and attractions, there are lots more off-the-beaten-path wonders to explore:

- **Playa Manzanillo:** Escape the throng and travel to Playa Manzanillo, a peaceful beach situated north of Playa La Ropa. Here, you'll discover a calm seashore and a nice beachside restaurant offering wonderful seafood.

- **Playa Troncones**: Just up the coast, Troncones is a tranquil beach town noted for its great surfing conditions and laid-back ambience. It's a perfect site for a day excursion or an overnight stay.

- **Las Pozas de Cacaluta:** Discover these secret freshwater ponds buried away in the woods near Zihuatanejo. Hiking to Las Pozas is an excursion that rewards you with a cool plunge in natural pools.

- **Mercado de Mariscos**: Visit the seafood market in downtown Zihuatanejo in the morning to observe local fishermen bringing in their daily catch. You may purchase fresh fish to cook or eat at a local restaurant.

- **Cerro del Vigia:** Hike to Cerro del Vigia for panoramic views of Zihuatanejo Bay. It's a calm respite from the busy town below, and you can enjoy spectacular sunsets.

9.2. Saving Money on Your Trip

Traveling on a budget doesn't mean compromising experiences. Here are methods to save money while enjoying everything that Zihuatanejo has to offer:

- **Local Eateries:** Savor inexpensive and excellent meals at local taquerias, , and market stalls. Street cuisine and tiny family-run eateries frequently provide the greatest value.

- **Public Transportation**: Utilize local buses, or "combis," to go throughout town and adjacent regions. They are a cheap way to explore.

- **Haggle at Markets**: When shopping at markets, don't hesitate to haggle costs, particularly when purchasing souvenirs or crafts. Polite haggling is a widespread behavior.

- **Free Beach Activities**: Enjoy the beach without additional charges. Swim, sunbathe, or enjoy a stroll along the coastline without the need for pricey activities.

- **Happy Hours:** Many pubs and restaurants offer happy hour promotions on beverages and snacks. Take advantage of these offers for a more budget-friendly evening out.

9.3. Sustainable Travel Practices

Zihuatanejo's natural beauty is worth conserving. Here are ideas to conduct sustainable travel during your visit:

- **Reduce Plastic Use:** Bring a reusable water bottle and shopping bag to reduce plastic waste. Many companies in Zihuatanejo are taking initiatives to decrease single-use plastics.

- **Respect Wildlife**: When snorkeling, keep a respectful distance from marine life and coral reefs. Avoid touching or upsetting aquatic organisms.

- **Support Local:** Choose locally-owned motels, restaurants, and stores to contribute to the local economy. Seek for firms that promote sustainability and environmental responsibility.

- **Conserve Water and Energy:** Use water and electricity carefully in your accommodation. Turn off lights and air conditioning when not in use and opt for brief showers to save water.

- **Leave No Trace**: Practice Leave No Trace principles while hiking or visiting natural places. Carry out all rubbish and leave the environment as you find it.

Zihuatanejo provides a treasure trove of experiences for every tourist, whether you're hunting hidden jewels, hoping to save money, or aiming to be a responsible and sustainable traveler. This insider advice will help you make the most of your Zihuatanejo vacation while having a beneficial influence on the environment and local people.

Chapter 10: TRAVEL ITINERARY

10.1. A Week in Zihuatanejo

Zihuatanejo provides a week-long trip loaded with different activities, from beach days to cultural discovery. Here's a recommended itinerary to make the most of your stay:

Day 1: Arrival and Exploration

- Arrive at Zihuatanejo-Ixtapa International Airport and travel to your hotel.
- Spend your first day visiting the town. Stroll down Paseo del Pescador and eat at a neighborhood restaurant.
- Catch a magnificent sunset over Zihuatanejo Bay.

Day 2: Beach Day

- Head to Playa La Ropa for a relaxed day on the beach. Swim, sunbathe, and enjoy the pristine waters.
- Savor seafood at a coastal restaurant for lunch.
- In the afternoon, visit Playa Principal for a boat trip or a walk along the crowded promenade.

Day 3: Water Adventures

- Try an exciting aquatic experience like snorkeling or scuba diving to discover marine life and coral reefs.
- Have lunch at a seafood restaurant.
- Enjoy an evening boat cruise with meals and live music on board.

Day 4: Cultural Exploration

- Explore Zihuatanejo's cultural treasures, beginning with a visit to the Iglesia de Nuestra Señora de Guadalupe.
- Explore the Mercado de Artesanías for unique gifts.
- Attend a local dance or music performance in the evening.

Day 5: Day Trip to Ixtapa

- Take a day excursion to Ixtapa, Zihuatanejo's adjacent vacation town.
- Visit Playa El Palmar for beach activities and watersports.
- Explore the Marina Ixtapa and have lunch at one of its beachfront restaurants.
- Return to Zihuatanejo in the evening.

Day 6: Relaxation and Shopping

- Spend a peaceful morning on the beach or treat yourself with a spa day.
- Explore the town's stores for souvenirs, jewelry, and local crafts.
- Dine at one of Zihuatanejo's international or local restaurants.

Day 7: Farewell and Departure

- Enjoy your final morning in Zihuatanejo with a substantial breakfast.
- Take a last stroll along the beach or see any last-minute sites.
- Check out of your lodging and go to the airport for your departure.
- This programme provides a wonderful balance of leisure, adventure, and cultural discovery during your week in Zihuatanejo. Of course, feel free to

customize it depending on your choices and interests to build your perfect Zihuatanejo experience.

Chapter 11: TRAVEL ITINERARY- EXTENDED STAY

For those lucky enough to prolong their stay in Zihuatanejo, tailoring your schedule offers a superb chance to dig further into the region's beauty and culture. Here's some advice on how to make the most of an extended stay:

Week 1-2: Beach Retreat

- Begin with a week of pure leisure. Choose various beaches each day to truly experience Zihuatanejo's coastline variety.
- Dedicate time to aquatic activities like paddleboarding, kayaking, and beachcombing.

- Delight in seafood at several beachside palapas, experiencing new tastes every day.

Week 3: Exploring Nature and Wildlife

- Explore the rich natural surroundings with jungle walks or excursions to local wildlife parks.
- Embark on wildlife trips, including bird-watching or a trip to view sea turtle hatching (seasonal).
- Dine at restaurants with forest or coastal views to immerse yourself in the region's splendor.

Week 4: Cultural Immersion

- Dive deeper into the local culture by taking Spanish language courses or engaging in traditional cookery workshops.

- Attend local festivals or festivities, if they overlap with your longer stay.
- Volunteer or join in community activities to give back to the local community.

Week 5-6: Day Trips and Exploration

- Dedicate these weeks to day trips and excursions, like returning to Ixtapa for a fresh experience or seeing off-the-beaten-path villages like Petatlán.
- Discover additional hidden treasures and indulge in adventurous activities like horseback riding, fishing, or visiting surrounding islands.
- Enjoy relaxed nights with live music and cultural acts.

Week 7: Sustainability and Conservation

- Immerse yourself in eco-tourism, such as participating in beach cleanups or visiting environmental conservation initiatives.
- Take part in responsible tourist activities, such as learning about sea turtle conservation initiatives or the preservation of the local flora and animals.
- Conclude your longer vacation with a deeper respect for Zihuatanejo's natural beauty.

This extended stay schedule enables you to truly engage with Zihuatanejo's nature, culture, and community. Whether it's relaxing on its gorgeous beaches, immersing yourself in local customs, or helping to preserve its natural beauties, Zihuatanejo's prolonged stay provides a meaningful and unique experience.

Chapter 12: TRANSPORTATION

Navigating Zihuatanejo and reaching this beachfront beauty is a vital element of your vacation. Here's a detailed guide to transportation alternatives in and around Zihuatanejo:

12.1 Getting to Zihuatanejo

- **By Air:** The most frequent method to reach Zihuatanejo is by flying into Zihuatanejo-Ixtapa International Airport (ZIH). This airport is well-connected to major Mexican cities and provides international flights. From the airport, you may take a cab or shuttle to your hotel in Zihuatanejo.

- **By Bus**: Zihuatanejo is accessible by bus from numerous Mexican cities, including Mexico City, Acapulco, and Puerto Vallarta. Long-distance buses are comfortable and provide many degrees of service. The bus station is conveniently positioned in the center.

- **By Car:** If you prefer a road journey, you may drive to Zihuatanejo. The community is accessible by the picturesque Highway 200. Keep in mind that the travel may be lengthy, and road conditions may fluctuate, so plan appropriately.

12.2. Local Transportation Options

- **Taxis**: Taxis are frequently accessible in Zihuatanejo and are a handy method to navigate about the area. Fares are normally affordable, but it's essential to settle on a price with the driver before beginning your trip.

- **Local Buses (Combis):** Zihuatanejo has a network of local buses known as "combis." These compact vans offer a cheap method to travel throughout the town and to adjacent locations like Ixtapa. They follow established routes and are a frequent means of transportation for residents and tourists alike.

- **Rental Bicycles:** Many hotels and rental businesses provide bicycles for touring Zihuatanejo. It's a pleasant and eco-friendly method to navigate the town and local beaches.

- **Strolling**: Zihuatanejo's town center and beach sections are pedestrian-friendly, making strolling a delightful way to explore the town's sights, shops, and restaurants.

12.3. Car Rentals and Driving Tips

If you want to hire a vehicle during your stay in Zihuatanejo, consider the following:

- **Rental Agencies**: Several international and local automobile rental businesses operate in Zihuatanejo, and you may book rentals at the airport or in town.

- **Driving in Mexico**: Driving in Mexico is on the right side of the road, and traffic signs are generally in Spanish. Be prepared for diverse driving traditions and local traffic restrictions. Ensure you have the required insurance coverage.

- **Parking**: Most motels in Zihuatanejo have parking facilities. In the town center, you'll find parking lots and on-street parking, however, it might become congested at peak periods.

- **Road Conditions**: Roads in and around Zihuatanejo are typically in decent condition, but it's recommended to check road conditions and plan your routes, particularly if you're going on lengthy excursions.

- **Gas Stations:** Fuel up at established gas stations, since they are more trustworthy than roadside sellers. Carry cash for petrol, since some stations may not take credit cards.

Understanding your transportation options and making the appropriate selections assures a seamless and pleasurable experience while touring Zihuatanejo and its neighboring regions. Whether you prefer flying, driving, or utilizing local transit, Zihuatanejo is fairly accessible and provides several methods to get about.

Chapter 13: TRAVEL TIPS FOR 2024

As you plan your vacation to Zihuatanejo in 2024, it's crucial to be updated about any updates or changes that may have happened since your previous visit in 2023. Here are some crucial aspects to consider:

13.1. Updates & Changes in 2023

- **COVID-19 procedures:** Check the current COVID-19 travel regulations and procedures for Zihuatanejo. Regulations may vary, so be prepared to follow any entrance, testing, or immunization requirements.

- **Accommodation**: Verify the status of hotels and resorts, since some may have undergone renovations or changes of ownership. Ensure your selected lodging is open and operating.

- **Restaurant and Business Closures**: Due to economic causes or unanticipated situations, several restaurants and businesses may have closed since your previous visit. Check for the newest suggestions and reviews to find new eating alternatives.

- **Transportation**: Confirm the availability and scheduling of flights, buses, and transportation services. Some routes or services may have been altered.

- **Events and Festivals:** Zihuatanejo's events and festival schedule may have changed. Check the dates and details of any festivities or cultural events you want to attend.

13.2. Seasonal Recommendations

- **Weather Considerations:** Zihuatanejo enjoys a tropical environment, with the dry season usually from November to April and the rainy season from May to October. Plan your vacation according to your weather preferences, bearing in mind that the dry season is often the most popular period for travelers.

- **Whale Watching**: If you're interested in whale watching, come during the winter months, from December to April, when humpback whales travel to the region. Consider taking a whale-watching excursion for an amazing experience.

- **Sea Turtle Nesting**: If you're serious about animal protection, schedule your vacation around sea turtle nesting season, which happens from June to November. You may join in nightly sea turtle releases arranged by local conservation organizations.

- **Festivals and Events**: Research the festival schedule for 2024 to match your visit with any specific events or festivities that interest you. Events like the Zihuatanejo International Guitar Festival and cultural festivals provide unique experiences.

- **Booking in Advance**: As tourism in Zihuatanejo continues to increase, it's important to book lodgings, excursions, and transportation in advance, particularly during busy tourist seasons. This assures availability and maybe better pricing.

By keeping up-to-date with travel developments and following seasonal advice, you can make the most of your vacation to Zihuatanejo in 2024. Whether you're seeking sunny days on the beach, cultural immersion, or natural adventures, Zihuatanejo provides a plethora of chances to make unforgettable memories.

Chapter 14: RESOURCES AND CONTACTS

When going to Zihuatanejo, it's vital to have access to useful information and emergency contacts to guarantee a safe and pleasurable journey. Here's a selection of valuable websites, applications, and critical emergency contacts:

14.1. Useful Websites and Apps:

- **Google Maps**: This software helps navigate the streets of Zihuatanejo, locate sights, and obtain directions to your destination, whether by foot or automobile.

- **Weather.com:** Stay current on Zihuatanejo's weather conditions and predictions. Knowing the weather may help you plan activities and prepare properly.

- **XE currencies Converter**: If you need to convert currencies, this app gives real-time exchange rate information, helping you manage your finances while in Zihuatanejo.

- **TripAdvisor:** Check this website or app for user reviews, ratings, and suggestions for hotels, restaurants, and activities in Zihuatanejo.

- **WhatsApp**: Stay in touch with friends, family, and local connections using WhatsApp, a frequently used messaging software in Mexico.

- **iOverlander**: If you're planning a road trip or camping experience, iOverlander gives information about campsites, parking areas, and facilities across Mexico.

- **Zihuatanejo tourist Website**: Visit the official Zihuatanejo tourist website for information on local attractions, events, and travel recommendations. It's a wonderful resource for arranging your vacation.

14.2. Emergency Contacts:

- **Emergency Services:** For any emergency circumstance, phone 911. This number links you to the local authorities, including police, fire, and medical services.

- **Tourist Police**: Zihuatanejo has a designated Tourist Police team that may help travelers with numerous difficulties. Their phone is +52 755 554 8585.

- **Medical Emergencies**: In case of a medical emergency, proceed to the closest hospital or clinic. The Hospital General de Zihuatanejo is a well-equipped medical center in the region. Their contact information is +52 755 554 0000.

- **U.S. Embassy and Consulate:** If you're a U.S. citizen and want help, the closest U.S. Embassy and Consulate is in Mexico City. The contact information is +52 55 8526 2561.

- **Canadian Embassy and Consulate**: For Canadian citizens requesting help, the closest Canadian Embassy and Consulate are in Mexico City. The contact information is +52 55 5724 7900.

- **Local Pharmacies:** Pharmacies are plentiful in Zihuatanejo. Farmacias Similares and Farmacias Guadalajara are two well-known drugstore businesses. Keep their contact information ready for non-emergency medical needs.

Having access to these services and emergency contacts guarantees that you may traverse Zihuatanejo with confidence and request help in case of any unanticipated difficulties. With the correct knowledge on your hands, your vacation to this lovely seaside region may be both safe and pleasurable.

Chapter 15: CONCLUSION AND FAREWELL

As your Zihuatanejo travel guide draws to an end, we hope that this thorough resource has given you vital insights and information to plan an amazing vacation to this charming seaside town. Zihuatanejo is a place that elegantly mixes the beauty of a typical Mexican fishing community with the draw of gorgeous beaches, rich culture, and kind hospitality.

In Zihuatanejo, you may bask in the golden sun on magnificent beaches, devour wonderful seafood, immerse yourself in the local culture, and make unforgettable memories. Whether you're seeking leisure, adventure, or cultural discovery, Zihuatanejo provides everything.

Remember to remain current on travel warnings and COVID-19 rules to ensure a safe and happy visit. Whether you're beginning a week-long holiday, an extended stay, or returning to find new adventures, Zihuatanejo welcomes you with open arms.

As you say goodbye to this book, we wish you a lovely voyage filled with amazing experiences, magnificent sunsets, and the warm embrace of Zihuatanejo's beauty. May your journey in this seaside paradise be all you've dreamt of and more. Safe travels and hasta !

Zihuatanejo

94

Zihuatanejo

Made in the USA
Monee, IL
10 December 2024

73245453R00056